M000291513

"In Luke 11:1, the disciples ask Jesu
very likely, these men had seen pe
participated in traditional prayers. 1
of times and seen people pray. But they didn't know how to pray? Perhaps their
request of Jesus was not as much from a position of ignorance, but because
Jesus's prayers were different from anything they had seen or experienced. Jesus
didn't just pray—He communed with the Father. He spoke out of relationship, not
pride. This is what the disciples longed for. They weren't desiring to learn to pray;
they desired to pray as Jesus did. As you engage in this *40-Day Prayer Journal*,
do more than engage in the discipline of prayer. Use this as an opportunity to
deepen your relationship with the Father. The outlines, prompts, and text will
provide a foundation for the Holy Spirit to enrich the time you spend in prayer.
Perhaps this will be the most transformative 40 days of your life."

—**Mark Entzminger,** *National Director of Children's*
Ministries, General Council of the Assemblies of God

"Once again, Josh has created something incredibly helpful and practical. The
simplicity of it is exactly why you can—and should—use the *40-Day Prayer*
Journal. Whether you've always struggled with prayer, or you simply want to
grow in the depth of your prayer life, grab a copy and let it guide you into a
greater sense of intimacy and relationship with a Father who not only knows you
but wants to be known by you."

—**Keith Ferrin**, *Author, Speaker, Creator of "Bible-Life Community"*

"Praying the Scriptures is a powerful tool for aligning our wills to the will of the
Father. Through a practical format and insightful guidance, Josh has provided
leaders with a grace-filled tool for daily encounters with the Lord in prayer. If you
want to step deeper into your faith and fellowship with Jesus, consider taking this
40-day journey."

—**Michayla White,** *Executive Director of the*
International Network of Children's Ministry

LEADVOLUNTEERS

PRAYER JOURNAL

> *A 40-DAY JOURNEY THROUGH PRAYING THE SCRIPTURES*

JOSH DENHART

CONTENTS

Introduction vii

PART 1 - DAYS 1-10
God Answers Prayer 14

Day #1 – The Upside-Down Kingdom 16

Day #2 – A Paradoxical Kingdom 18

Day #3 – Serving in an Upside-Down Kingdom 20

Day #4 – Gifts for the Giving 22

Day #5 – Fervor and Zeal 24

Day #6 – Kingdom Math 26

Day #7 – Water Out; Water In 28

Day #8 – One Handful vs. Two Fistfuls 30

Day #9 – His Eyes are Searching 32

Day #10 – Grace for Something...Not Nothing 34

PART 2 - DAYS 11-20
Ask God, He Gives Generously 38

Day #11 – Redeeming the Wrongs of Others 40

Day #12 – Loving the Hard Ones 42

Day #13 – The Everybody Kingdom 44

Day #14 – Persevere and Sow Seeds 46

Day #15 – Secretly Shouldering the Load 48

Day #16 – The Kingdom Value of Unity 50

Day #17 – Friendly Fire 52

Day #18 – Entrusting This One to Him 54

Day #19 - Keep Your Antennas High 56

Day #20 - Today is a Choice 58

PART 3 · DAYS 21-30

Overcoming Spiritual Paralysis...................................... 62

    Day #21 – Here Am I, Again.................................... 64

    Day #22 – Making the Team.................................... 66

    Day #23 – Flies on the Screen................................. 68

    Day #24 – Ministry is a Lifestyle, Not a Job........................ 70

    Day #25 – The Right DNA...................................... 72

    Day #26 – Knowing God Through Experience 74

    Day #27 – Power to Persevere 76

    Day #28 – Don't Be a Ball Hog 78

    Day #29 – Who Gets the Glory? 80

    Day #30 – Every Single Thing.................................. 82

PART 4 · DAYS 31-40

The Harvest is Plentiful... 86

    Day #31 – Home Base... 88

    Day #32 – The Gravitas of Action............................... 90

    Day #33- Being a Builder 92

    Day #34 – God Does Not Forget............................... 94

    Day #35 – A Lovely Reputation 96

    Day #36 – Work Takes Work 98

    Day #37 – Know the Right Things 100

    Day #38 – Faithful in Little 102

    Day #39 – Muscle Memory 104

    Day #40 – The Double Bonus 106

Conclusion: No Need for Anxiety.................................... 108

INTRODUCTION

IT'S ABOUT THE GOSPEL

Regardless of our specific ministry contexts, we all have projects, programs or events that require huge amounts of effort. It can feel overwhelming at times. In the midst of it all, in the quietness of our hearts, we will inevitably ask ourselves, "What is the point?" Well, it is the Gospel.

Our labor is for the Good News of Jesus Christ. We organize for the opportunity to proclaim salvation. We recruit and rally a regiment of moms, dads, senior saints and seniors in high school to one end: The Gospel. Our drive, our determination and our dedication are singularly directed: **It** is the Gospel. The fun is a bonus. The laughter from game-playing is a joyful noise. The challenge of scheduling is an outlet for our well-managed OCD. And —in a weird way —we love it.

Yet, when it is all said and done, it **IS** about the Gospel. Our songs point to the cross. Our prayers are ratcheted up a notch. Our hearts swell as we see impromptu gatherings of volunteers in prayer. We all want nothing more than the message of Jesus to be clearly communicated to our community. It is about **the** Gospel. The Gospel compels me. It is the "why" behind every late-night push, the fuel behind every conquered roadblock, and the prize at the end of this race. It is about the **GOSPEL**.

"May we never forget the promises found in Scripture concerning our efforts. "Nothing you do in the Lord is in vain."
—1 CORINTHIANS 15:58

HOW TO USE THE LEAD VOLUNTEERS PRAYER GUIDE

This prayer guide follows a simple pathway to help you to connect with God. Using just one verse per day, we will seek to center our hearts—to learn how to "Pray the Scriptures" through this guided meditation.

Years ago, I learned a powerful way to "Pray the Scriptures." This simple yet profound practice allows me to glean content for my prayer life directly from one verse of the Bible.

Each day, you will follow three steps:

Read

Record

Reconnect

#1 – Read: Read the verse and the following short meditation on the left-hand pages.

#2 – Record: Based on the verse of the day, record a thought under the **P.R.A.Y.** acronym.

> **P**raise - What Can I **Praise** God About Today?
>
> **R**eset - What Items Need a **Reset,** or My **Repentance,** Today?
>
> **A**sk - What Requests Could I **Ask** of God Today?
>
> **Y**ield - How Can I Assume a Posture of Submission Toward God Today?

#3 – Reconnect: Using the verse and your reflections, pray aloud or in your heart to the Lord.

We have provided an example on the next page.

EXAMPLE – GOD DOES NOT FORGET

HEBREWS 6:10
"God is not unjust; he will not forget your work and the love you have shown him as you have helped his people and continue to help them."

God sees, God knows and God is waiting with reward for you. He is NOT unjust! God does not forget. While you have likely forgotten some of your own times of faithfulness and labor, the Lord has not. God is all-knowing (omniscient). God is all-powerful (omnipotent). God is everywhere (omnipresent). We are omni-nothing. God is omni-everything. He sees all. He remembers all His children's works. Worship Him, because He does NOT forget our labors. We as humans, however, do forget. We have all overlooked a volunteer's labor and their contributions. Sometimes and somehow, our best volunteers' efforts have sadly gone unnoticed by us. But God, being good, does not forget our work for the Kingdom. None of our efforts in the Lord are unaccounted for or missed. Who should you pour into today, knowing that God will never forget how you seek to help the saints? In addition, who should you call today to thank for their labors in the Lord? Someone may need reminding that God has been noticing and keeping track of all their love and labor!

REFLECT

Praise - *What Can I Praise God About Today?*

I praise you God, because you are just. You, Lord, don't forget our work for you. Thank you for keeping track of our labors and toils.

Reset - *What Items Need a Reset in My Life Today?*

God, I sometimes grow weary as I seek to serve your people. Sometimes, I feel resentful and think I am alone. You keep track, and I don't want to forget that. I am serving you as I serve them.

Ask - *What Requests Could I Ask of God Today?*

Lord, help me remember that you are cheering me on and keeping track of all of my hard work. Please help me keep my "treasures in heaven," and pleasing you, top-of-mind today.

Yield - *How Can I Assume a Posture of Submission Toward God Today?*

Father, I am but one person. I cannot do it all. You know this. Please help me to do my part today in your kingdom. Help me be mindful as I labor today, remembering that you know all and will reward.

RECONNECT

PART 1

DAYS 1-10

GOD ANSWERS PRAYER

God answers prayer. This is His job. He is capable. He is strong enough. He is wise enough to know if our prayer is a prayer worthy of being answered. That is His job. Only He can do it.

My job —simply put —is to pray. Paul prayed for opportunity. Paul prayed for clear words. Paul prayed for the hearts of others to be opened. Paul prayed for doors to be opened. Paul prayed for all the members of the body to work together in unity for one purpose: The Gospel Message. We pray; God hears. Those are the roles. Those are our jobs.

I *cannot* answer prayer! That is exclusively God's domain. The trick is to recognize what my role is and how to depend upon Him for His role.

We pray. We entrust our needs to the Lord. We seek to do our part, and then we go to bed. I can sleep well at night having done my job, because I am partnered in ministry with the One who does never sleeps nor slumbers. He is constantly at work. He does not need us, but He desires to use us. We exist in partnership with Him. I love Him. I deeply trust Him. I want to continue to grow in my trust in Him.

Ask yourself this humbling question: Are you praying for the salvation of the kids, students and adults in your ministry? You may emphatically say, "Yes, of course!" However, let's not fool ourselves. I was a children's pastor for over 10 years, and I can honestly say that I found myself working for and praying for far lesser things. I was in charge of a huge ministry. I found myself seeking to solve important but lower-level things. I was solving organizational and tactical issues, often to the exclusion of the most important things!

Jesus commanded us to pray. Check out this passage that reveals the heart of Jesus in Matthew 9: *"Seeing the people, He felt compassion for them, because they were distressed and dispirited like sheep without a shepherd. Then He said to His disciples, 'The harvest is plentiful, but the workers are few. Therefore pray to the Lord of the harvest to send out workers into His harvest.'"*

We want workers; we pray for volunteers...but to what end? Well, because people are distressed, like sheep without a shepherd. People need the Lord. Our goal in finding volunteers should be singular in focus: For people to hear the gospel. God answers prayer; we simply pray.

DAY #1 – THE UPSIDE-DOWN KINGDOM

MATTHEW 23:11

"The greatest among you will be your servant."

True greatness is helping others toward greatness. When Jesus said, "The greatest among you will be your servant," He was ushering in the Upside-Down Kingdom. Do you want to be first? Be last. Do you want to be rich? Give away. Do you want to live? Die. Do you want to be exalted? Choose humility. This is the Upside-Down Kingdom. People who work according to the rules of the "kingdom of this world" will step on others so that they can be great. In contrast, believers who operate according to the rules of the Upside-Down Kingdom allow their lives to be stepping-stones for the lowly to climb toward greatness. The "kingdom of this world" exalts self: speed, beauty and power. The Upside-Down Kingdom exalts others: the slow, the awkward and the powerless. Residents of the "kingdom of this world" fear becoming a doormat and do not want anyone to tread on them. Residents in the Upside-Down Kingdom allow others to stand on their shoulders and rise. Which of these kingdoms will you reside in today? Whom can you elevate today?

REFLECT

*P*raise - *What Can I Praise God About Today?*

_____

_____

_____

*R*eset - *What Items Need a Reset in My Life Today?*

_____

_____

_____

*A*sk - *What Requests Could I Ask of God Today?*

_____

_____

_____

*Y*ield - *How Can I Assume a Posture of Submission Toward God Today?*

_____

_____

_____

RECONNECT

_____

_____

_____

_____

_____

DAY #2 – A PARADOXICAL KINGDOM

LUKE 6:38

"Give, and it will be given to you. A good measure, pressed down, shaken together and running over, will be poured into your lap. For with the measure you use, it will be measured to you."

The beauty of the "Upside-Down Kingdom" is the paradox of it all. When we give, we somehow find that we have more. We empty ourselves, only to find that we are filled. However, it's not that our giving entitles us to payback. God owes us nothing. Rather, this Upside-Down Kingdom of God has a multifaceted reward system. We may give our gold and silver, yet our reward comes in peace and contentment. We may give our time and toil, yet our reward comes in deeper kingdom relationships. We may pour out our hearts and counsel, yet God rewards us with an overflowing emotional reserve. Remember: you cannot out-give God. His rewards are perfectly-timed and often wonderfully mysterious. Give big. Give your treasure, your time and your toil. Live with an expectant view that God cannot wait to give back unto you. Give to those you lead today. Who can you reach out to and bless today? Your limited time is a prized commodity. Share it, and see what happens.

REFLECT

*P*raise - What Can I Praise God About Today?

_____

_____

_____

*R*eset - What Items Need a Reset in My Life Today?

_____

_____

_____

*A*sk - What Requests Could I Ask of God Today?

_____

_____

_____

*Y*ield - How Can I Assume a Posture of Submission Toward God Today?

_____

_____

_____

RECONNECT

_____

_____

_____

_____

_____

DAY #3 — SERVING IN AN UPSIDE-DOWN KINGDOM

MARK 10:45

"For even the Son of Man did not come to be served, but to serve, and to give his life as a ransom for many."

Jesus is the King of this "Upside-Down Kingdom." He held a high position. Though He was worshiped by angels from all eternity past, He took on human flesh and washed the feet of sinful humans. "Wait," You might say. "You mean the King of the Universe washed feet? That sounds backwards." This is the way of the Upside-Down. Jesus is our example. The highest King took up the lowest towel. Any elevated position you hold in the Upside-Down Kingdom of God is given to you so that you can make life better and easier for someone else. Do you see your position as an opportunity to help someone have a richer life experience? Or do you see your position merely as a justification for others to make life easier for you? Doing ministry according to the Upside-Down is hard. Serving will cost us. It certainly cost Jesus His very life. Take a moment and examine what advantages you can provide to another person through your limited position and authority. You were granted your post to support those under you, not the other way around. How can you make life better for someone else today?

REFLECT

*P*raise - What Can I Praise God About Today?

_____

_____

_____

*R*eset - What Items Need a Reset in My Life Today?

_____

_____

_____

*A*sk - What Requests Could I Ask of God Today?

_____

_____

_____

*Y*ield - How Can I Assume a Posture of Submission Toward God Today?

_____

_____

_____

RECONNECT

_____

_____

_____

_____

_____

DAY #4 – GIFTS FOR THE GIVING

1 PETER 4:10
"Each one should use whatever gift he has received to serve others, faithfully administering God's grace in its various forms."

In the Upside-Down Kingdom of God, our gifts are for the giving. We were endowed with gifts. However, the intent of the gift is not to bless us alone. The intent of the gift is to liberally use it to serve someone else. Do you have a gift? If you are a child of God, you certainly do. God has bestowed at least one spiritual gift on each of His children. His gifts are rather varied, though, aren't they? It seems that some people receive a cornucopia of gifts, while others receive fewer. The name of the game is to recognize the gifts you have and not fret about the ones you lack. Are you resentful of the gifts of others? Longing for gifts you don't have is a futile waste. Regardless of the number or even quality of the gifts, all of them are given for one purpose: to serve others. You received your gifts from Him. You are using them for Him. First, do you know what they are? Secondly, are there people around you who need your gifts today? Thirdly, can you spot someone else's gift today and thank them for it? Thank you for using YOUR gifts!

REFLECT

*P*raise - *What Can I Praise God About Today?*

_____

_____

_____

*R*eset - *What Items Need a Reset in My Life Today?*

_____

_____

_____

*A*sk - *What Requests Could I Ask of God Today?*

_____

_____

_____

*Y*ield - *How Can I Assume a Posture of Submission Toward God Today?*

_____

_____

_____

RECONNECT

_____

_____

_____

_____

_____

DAY #5 – FERVOR AND ZEAL

2 CORINTHIANS 9:7-8
"Each one must give as he has decided in his heart, not reluctantly or under compulsion, for God loves a cheerful giver. And God is able to make all grace abound to you, so that having all sufficiency in all things at all times, you may abound in every good work."

Giving encompasses many things, including time, treasure and talent. Paul encourages believers to sacrifice financially, which will result in them having less. There are "costs" to giving financially. Yet God is the King of this "Upside-Down Kingdom," and He abounds in resources. Our giving does not leave us destitute, but rather amply supplied. As leaders in ministry, we give a lot. We place our time, our toil and talents on His altar. There are "costs" to giving yourself to ministry. These costs include sacrifices of family, freedoms and more. However, we have a choice. We can be cheerful givers, or the alternative. This is your one and only life. You will be in heaven one day, and all the work will be finished. Now is the time to work and labor cheerfully. God will not leave you destitute but amply supplied in areas far beyond your finances. Today is a choice: give cheerfully.

REFLECT

Praise - What Can I Praise God About Today?

_____

_____

_____

Reset - What Items Need a Reset in My Life Today?

_____

_____

_____

Ask - What Requests Could I Ask of God Today?

_____

_____

_____

Yield - How Can I Assume a Posture of Submission Toward God Today?

_____

_____

_____

RECONNECT

_____

_____

_____

_____

_____

DAY #6 – KINGDOM MATH

ACTS 20:35

"And remember the words of the Lord Jesus, that He said, 'It is more blessed to give than to receive.'"

Do you remember the children's book Counting Apples, that featured three cartoon animals balancing apples on their heads? This "pre-math" book for toddlers visually displays, more or less, apples and sing-song-rhymes. Soon, our kids advanced to formal addition, subtraction and beyond. It was not until I was an adult that I learned "Kingdom Math." Up to this point, giving apples meant I had less and getting apples meant I had more. Yet Acts 20:35 showcases a new math, a "Kingdom Math." Solomon agrees, adding, "Give of the first of all you produce...so that your barns will overflow with plenty" (Proverbs 3:9-10). What an interesting if-then clause. Do you want "better?" Do you want "overflow?" Give some apples, and see what the next pages hold. This is not just a saying or a simple colloquialism. This is the "Upside-Down Kingdom." This Kingdom has different equations. Today, give yourself, your treasure, and your talents. Experience Kingdom Math at work.

REFLECT

*P*raise - *What Can I Praise God About Today?*

_____

_____

_____

*R*eset - *What Items Need a Reset in My Life Today?*

_____

_____

_____

*A*sk - *What Requests Could I Ask of God Today?*

_____

_____

_____

*Y*ield - *How Can I Assume a Posture of Submission Toward God Today?*

_____

_____

_____

RECONNECT

_____

_____

_____

_____

_____

DAY #7 – WATER OUT; WATER IN

PROVERBS 11:25

"The one who waters will himself be watered."

Ministry is a process of continually giving. Sometimes, we feel insecure about pouring out, because we fear becoming empty. We can be blessing-hoarders. We don't water others out of fear that our cups will become bone-dry. Yet God keeps His word. Continuing to water others is a matter of faith. Which happens first: my giving or my refilling? Herein lies yet another lesson in the "Upside-Down Kingdom of God." It all begins with letting the waters of refreshment flow from me. In faith, I water; then, I find God bringing new waters to refresh my soul. I want water to flow into me—therefore, I allow water to leave me and bless others. I water, and then I am watered. God faithfully comes behind me with waters of refreshment. I have sought to refresh people, and I eagerly anticipate God to refresh me. I have watered other people's children, and am banking on God to water mine. I do not want to be a stagnant and stale holding tank of water; therefore, I begin by watering others. Every time I fill someone else's cup with cool water, I find that my water bucket is replenished. Who's around you that's parched? Whom can you water today?

REFLECT

*P*raise - What Can I Praise God About Today?

_____

_____

_____

*R*eset - What Items Need a Reset in My Life Today?

_____

_____

_____

*A*sk - What Requests Could I Ask of God Today?

_____

_____

_____

*Y*ield - How Can I Assume a Posture of Submission Toward God Today?

_____

_____

_____

RECONNECT

_____

_____

_____

_____

_____

_____

DAY #8 – ONE HANDFUL VS. TWO FISTFULS

ECCLESIASTES 4:6

***"One handful of rest is better than two fistfuls
of labor and striving after the wind."***

There is no end to the tasks our hands could find in ministry. There is always something more we think we could—or even should—do. Solomon's word choice draws a stark juxtaposition in my heart: "one handful" vs. "two fistfuls." I cherish my rest simply because I have learned to do so the hard way. With youthful zeal, I pursued a never-ending list of good things—often to my demise. These days, I am quite content to have one handful of rest and the other hand filled with labor. Yet so many ministry leaders injure themselves with "two fistfuls" of busyness and activity. Ministry is a long game, not a sprint. Just as the wise man stops to sharpen his axe, so a wise ministry leader knows the value of rest and Sabbath. Do you trust God? It sounds simplistic, doesn't it? But your ability to rest is in direct relationship to your trust in God's ability to further His ministry even while you sleep. The "Upside-Down Kingdom" understands the paradox of labor: God does more with my 6 days than I could do if I had 7 days. Can you pause and reaffirm that God cares more than you do about His ministry?

REFLECT

*P*raise - What Can I Praise God About Today?

_____

_____

_____

*R*eset - What Items Need a Reset in My Life Today?

_____

_____

_____

*A*sk - What Requests Could I Ask of God Today?

_____

_____

_____

*Y*ield - How Can I Assume a Posture of Submission Toward God Today?

_____

_____

_____

RECONNECT

_____

_____

_____

_____

_____

_____

DAY #9 – HIS EYES ARE SEARCHING

2 CHRONICLES 16:9
*"For the eyes of the LORD move to and fro
throughout the earth that He may strongly
support those whose heart is completely His."*

God is looking for someone. His eyes are searching across the earth. He is looking for someone to strongly support. Out of a sea of people, God is on the lookout for someone whose heart is completely His. The "Upside-Down Kingdom" values a committed heart more than a strong mind or back. If we want God's strong support, it begins with cultivating a heart wholly and unconditionally His. As the old hymn declares, "Prone to wander, Lord, I feel it." Having a heart that is completely His is an ongoing pursuit, a destination never reached. Hebrews 10:14 reads, "For by a single offering He has perfected for all time those who are being perfected." From a positional standpoint, we are perfect. From a process standpoint, we are being made perfect. Let not your heart be saddened, knowing that it is far from completely His. Pause today, raise your hand, and tell God that your heart is His—perfectly and imperfectly. Start today knowing that God's eyes are searching; His strong support awaits you.

REFLECT

Praise - What Can I Praise God About Today?

_____

_____

_____

Reset - What Items Need a Reset in My Life Today?

_____

_____

_____

Ask - What Requests Could I Ask of God Today?

_____

_____

_____

Yield - How Can I Assume a Posture of Submission Toward God Today?

_____

_____

_____

RECONNECT

_____

_____

_____

_____

_____

_____

DAY #10 – GRACE FOR SOMETHING...NOT NOTHING

2 CORINTHIANS 6:1

"As God's co-workers we urge you not to receive God's grace in vain."

Grace is defined as unmerited favor. God has given us His grace—He's bestowed favor on us, not because of our great worthiness, but purely out of His great love. One way in which we see God's grace is the gifts and abilities He's given to us. Beyond this, He allows us to work in His Kingdom. He gives us gifts; this is favor. I could have been given no gifts at all. God lets me work with Him; this is favor. I could have been sidelined. This verse, however, urges us to be fruitful, lest God's favor, or grace, be for nothing. In His grace, God gave us gifts. Will things be *better* because of those gifts? The term "in vain" means to go forth "without success or a result." I want the grace given to me to produce much fruit. God gave us something: let's not waste it. Are you being a fruitful worker? Are you laboring for Him out of love and gratitude for the grace He's given you? Let us march forth today with a renewed commitment to make good on the grace He has given. What unique gifts has He bestowed upon you? How has His favor been shown uniquely to you? You are a one-of-a-kind creation! May we never forget that God wants fruit from His investment.

REFLECT

*P*raise - What Can I Praise God About Today?

_____

_____

_____

*R*eset - What Items Need a Reset in My Life Today?

_____

_____

_____

*A*sk - What Requests Could I Ask of God Today?

_____

_____

_____

*Y*ield - How Can I Assume a Posture of Submission Toward God Today?

_____

_____

_____

RECONNECT

_____

_____

_____

_____

_____

_____

PART 2

DAYS 11-20

ASK GOD, HE GIVES GENEROUSLY

Taxes are complicated, right? I am not the greatest individual to entrust with mountains of detailed paperwork—especially tax-related paperwork. Therefore, the responsibility of filing my taxes gets outsourced to a professional.

Years ago, I called my tax guy with a simple question. One week later, I received an invoice in the mail for $80. A half-hour conversation about an item that really wasn't that important cost me $80! Initially, I was taken aback by this. Later, in a calmer state of mind, I came to realize that tax professionals are paid for their knowledge. I'd stepped into a relationship to gain knowledge from this person, and he needed to be paid accordingly. Now, however, I think long and hard before making any calls to him. I go to great lengths, including Google searches and reading, so as to not be put in a position where I'm penalized financially for asking a simple question.

He Doesn't Charge Us!

This negative experience with my tax professional has deeply influenced my spiritual life. The writer of James shows God in a stark contrast to this experience: God knows that we lack wisdom. He doesn't shame us for this or find fault with us. He doesn't charge us! God knows that we are but dust. We don't need to hesitate to ask God for wisdom. I realized that He is ready to provide me with spiritual wisdom. I don't need to wait to have all of the answers. I don't need to try to figure it out on my own for fear of looking like an idiot or being charged. God gives generously to all without finding fault. He gives spiritual wisdom freely. He just wants us to ask with faith and not doubt. God humbly says to us, "Please ask me. When you lack wisdom, just ask. I am not going to charge you, and I'm not going to find fault with you."

Ask God

I want to encourage you today: Whatever you're up against, simply ask God. Take time right now and present your requests to Him. Present your problems, and your lack of wisdom, to the Almighty God of the universe. If you're struggling with how to interact with a senior leader, ask God. Maybe you have a challenging volunteer you don't know how to engage. Ask God. When you're just not sure how you can reach the kids you are expected to reach with the woefully short monetary resources you have been entrusted with, ask God. If you lack knowledge regarding how to engage parents in the spiritual lives of their own children, ask God. He gives generously to all without finding fault.

Remember, at the end of the day, God does not charge you. He does not find fault in you. He gives generously to all. God simply wants you to ask.

As you enter into the next phase of this prayer journey, understand and own that access to God is available. His counsel and advice are free. Access to His wisdom is free. Asking Him to do something on your behalf does not cost you anything whatsoever.

God does not shame you. He does not scoff at your needy requests. He wants to help you. Remember these basic and profound truths.

DAY #11 – REDEEMING THE WRONGS OF OTHERS

LUKE 6:31

**"And as you wish that others would
do to you, do so to them."**

I was a volunteer for years before becoming a leader of volunteers. My experiences as a volunteer influenced how I lead them today. As a volunteer, I had both positive experiences and less positive experiences. I had leaders who cared deeply for me as a person, and leaders who blew me off and did not know me. Our interactions were polite, but transactional. Our relationship was based on what I did for them, not who I was to them. Those latter experiences hurt. Then, one day, I found myself as the leader. I now had a chance to treat volunteers the way I *wished* I had been treated. Those formerly painful memories became fuel. I got to retroactively right someone else's leadership wrongs. I felt empowered—filled with direction. Has someone ever lead you in a way that hurt you? I imagine the answer is yes. Has a leader ever made you feel like a widget instead of a worthy co-laborer? Sadly, we have all felt used. Can you leverage the wrongs of others? Yes, you can! Can the ways others have poorly lead or *are poorly leading you right now* influence how you lead others today? Absolutely. Let the pains of the past be fuel for today.

REFLECT

*P*raise - *What Can I Praise God About Today?*

_____

_____

_____

*R*eset - *What Items Need a Reset in My Life Today?*

_____

_____

_____

*A*sk - *What Requests Could I Ask of God Today?*

_____

_____

_____

*Y*ield - *How Can I Assume a Posture of Submission Toward God Today?*

_____

_____

_____

RECONNECT

_____

_____

_____

_____

_____

_____

DAY #12 – LOVING THE HARD ONES

LUKE 6:35
"But love your enemies, and do good, and lend,
expecting nothing in return, and your reward will
be great, and you will be sons of the Most High,
for he is kind to the ungrateful and the evil."

In life and in ministry, we will encounter different people. There are VCPs (Very Challenging People), VNPs (Very Needy People), and you might even run into some VAPs (Very Antagonistic People). Ministry is a high calling. We are called to "do good" with no expectation of earthly remuneration or recognition. Why do we do it? Why do we endure the misled, the mistaken and even those who seek to malign us? The Most High is our example. He is kind to the ungrateful and the evil. Thank you for your love to all as you serve. Your reward will be great. Can you think of a time or a situation where you were a VCP, a VNP, or even a VAP in someone else's life or ministry? When I consider the challenges I've brought to the lives of others, it gives me fuel to handle others with a greater measure of grace today. Who do you need to love today, regardless of their challenges to your life and ministry? Can you be kind to the ungrateful people around you today?

REFLECT

*P*raise - What Can I Praise God About Today?

_____

_____

_____

*R*eset - What Items Need a Reset in My Life Today?

_____

_____

_____

*A*sk - What Requests Could I Ask of God Today?

_____

_____

_____

*Y*ield - How Can I Assume a Posture of Submission Toward God Today?

_____

_____

_____

RECONNECT

_____

_____

_____

_____

_____

_____

DAY #13 – THE EVERYBODY KINGDOM

JAMES 2:1-2

"My brothers, show no partiality as you hold the faith in our Lord Jesus Christ, the Lord of glory. For if a man wearing a gold ring and fine clothing comes into your assembly, and a poor man in shabby clothing also comes in, do not treat them differently."

Some people are easy to love. We might call them VEPs (Very Encouraging People). As a leader, it's great when you are surrounded by VGPs (Very Gifted People) who can move our ministries forward. Somehow, our humanity is drawn to the VRPs (Very Rich People). However, the Kingdom of God is for everyone, not just the pretty people. The Kingdom is not only for the "Spiritual Navy Seals," "Discipleship Green Berets," and "Special Forces of the Faith." God warned us about our tendency to love *only* the easy, the gifted, or those we can enlist. The Kingdom of God is for those who have nothing to give. It has a special place for those who have nothing, from our perspective, to contribute. Thank you for loving all who cross your path today—not just the easy people, the rich people and the gifted people. This is an Everybody Kingdom. Who needs attention from you, despite what you think they can do for you? Call them. Reach out today.

REFLECT

*P*raise - *What Can I Praise God About Today?*

_____

_____

_____

*R*eset - *What Items Need a Reset in My Life Today?*

_____

_____

_____

*A*sk - *What Requests Could I Ask of God Today?*

_____

_____

_____

*Y*ield - *How Can I Assume a Posture of Submission Toward God Today?*

_____

_____

_____

RECONNECT

_____

_____

_____

_____

_____

_____

DAY #14 – PERSEVERE AND SOW SEEDS

GALATIANS 6:9-10

"And let us not grow weary of doing good, for in due season we will reap, if we do not give up. So then, as we have opportunity, let us do good to everyone, and especially to those who are of the household of faith."

Ministry is one of the loneliest "people jobs" in the world. People surround you, yet you cannot share some of the realities of your job. Your banker friend can share, "My boss is a train-wreck." Your bookkeeper friend can lament, "This company is going in a futile direction." However, your boss is their pastor, and the direction of your job is the direction of their church. It gets complicated quickly, doesn't it? There is a wearisome cost to serving the Lord that most do not understand. Doing good, especially to the faith-household, takes endurance. Seed-planting is the first step of a fruitful harvest. Yet seed germination can be slow. Some seeds sit dormant for a long time. Keep doing the good you are doing. Keep sowing seeds. Don't give up. Those who persevere will reap a harvest. Today, you will have opportunity to sow seeds. Keep your eyes on the dream of the harvest.

REFLECT

*P*raise - What Can I Praise God About Today?

_____

_____

_____

*R*eset - What Items Need a Reset in My Life Today?

_____

_____

_____

*A*sk - What Requests Could I Ask of God Today?

_____

_____

_____

*Y*ield - How Can I Assume a Posture of Submission Toward God Today?

_____

_____

_____

RECONNECT

_____

_____

_____

_____

_____

_____

DAY #15 – SECRETLY SHOULDERING THE LOAD

GALATIANS 6:2
"Bear one another's burdens, and
so fulfill the law of Christ."

Bearing burdens is a high calling. Every vocation has a unique set of "job hazards." Every career has associated risks. Doctors are exposed to disease; truckers are subject to dumb drivers; and lumberjacks run the risk of falling trees. Ministry has a unique set of job hazards, as well. Ministry is a people business. Everyone around you is carrying a secret, sacred burden. As shield-bearers for the Kingdom, one of our jobs is to notice heavy-laden sheep and shoulder some of their loads. Sheep, however, hide their lacerations from the flock. Our job is to know the flock, and to perceive even the smallest limp. As shepherds, our role is to bind the broken-hearted, comfort the weary and, yes, even take upon ourselves the load of another. Isn't this what Jesus did? "He who knew no sin, became sin for us..." (2 Corinthians 5:21). This is one of the many job hazards of ministry. Bearing the burden of another is hard, but it is good, fitting, and right. Are you willing to dig beneath the surface—to see invisible burdens? Will you enter into the hardship of another? Help someone today. Reach deeper. Support boldly. Bear a burden.

REFLECT

*P*raise - *What Can I Praise God About Today?*

_____

_____

_____

*R*eset - *What Items Need a Reset in My Life Today?*

_____

_____

_____

*A*sk - *What Requests Could I Ask of God Today?*

_____

_____

_____

*Y*ield - *How Can I Assume a Posture of Submission Toward God Today?*

_____

_____

_____

RECONNECT

_____

_____

_____

_____

_____

DAY #16 – THE KINGDOM VALUE OF UNITY

EPHESIANS 4:1-32
"I, therefore, a prisoner for the Lord, urge you to walk in a manner worthy of the calling to which you have been called, with all humility and gentleness, with patience, bearing with one another in love, eager to maintain the unity of the Spirit in the bond of peace."

As ministry leaders, we must delicately navigate leading the flock. The world prizes rash and unapologetically aggressive leaders. Ministry favors a posture of thoughtfulness, humility and gentleness. The world rewards running roughshod over the weak. Ministry favors those who tactfully leave no one behind as we guide the flock to higher ground. The world celebrates decisive action—even if it is divisive. Ministry cherishes unity as a Kingdom value. Which kingdom influences your leadership? Are you walking in a manner worthy of the Kingdom to which you have been called? Take your leadership cues from the Kingdom playbook, not from the ways of the worldly and unwise. Today, you have a calling to fulfill in the Kingdom. Therefore, operate under the values of this Kingdom. As you enter meetings, which kingdom are you representing? As you deal with people, solve problems and complete tasks, which kingdom dominates your actions?

REFLECT

*P*raise - What Can I Praise God About Today?

_____

_____

_____

*R*eset - What Items Need a Reset in My Life Today?

_____

_____

_____

*A*sk - What Requests Could I Ask of God Today?

_____

_____

_____

*Y*ield - How Can I Assume a Posture of Submission Toward God Today?

_____

_____

_____

RECONNECT

_____

_____

_____

_____

_____

_____

DAY #17 – FRIENDLY FIRE

2 TIMOTHY 2:24-26

"The Lord's bond-servant must not be quarrelsome, but be kind to all, able to teach, patient when wronged, with gentleness correcting those who are in opposition, if perhaps God may grant them repentance leading to the knowledge of the truth, and they may come to their senses and escape from the snare of the devil, having been held captive by him to do his will."

Ministry brings opinionated, and often demanding, people across our paths. Ministry demands an almost superhuman ability to deal with other human beings. God, help us to not be quarrelsome. Lord, help us to be kind to the person in our ministry who has wronged us. Allow us the wisdom and forbearance to teach and gently correct others while we are under personal attack. Ministry needs a tender-hearted leader who sees people as sheep, harassed and helpless, lacking a shepherd. This takes an extra measure of God's grace, especially when a friend does unfriendly things to you in the ministry. We are called to take up our cross. Today, bring your ministry wounds to the cross. Pray this passage today. Allow yourself to be grounded and grow to be like our Great Shepherd.

REFLECT

*P*raise - *What Can I Praise God About Today?*

_____

_____

_____

*R*eset - *What Items Need a Reset in My Life Today?*

_____

_____

_____

*A*sk - *What Requests Could I Ask of God Today?*

_____

_____

_____

*Y*ield - *How Can I Assume a Posture of Submission Toward God Today?*

_____

_____

_____

RECONNECT

_____

_____

_____

_____

_____

_____

DAY #18 – ENTRUSTING THIS ONE TO HIM

1 PETER 2:21-23
"For you have been called for this purpose, since Christ also suffered for you, leaving you an example for you to follow in His steps, who committed no sin, nor was any deceit found in His mouth; and while being reviled, He did not revile in return; while suffering, He uttered no threats, but kept entrusting Himself to Him who judges righteously.

Ministry is a ripe field for retribution and the desire to exact revenge. Those we serve sabotage our efforts, subvert our vision, and sever healthy relationships. We should not be shocked, since the Great Shepherd drank this bitter cup, too. As under-shepherds, we are called to "share in the suffering of Christ." Those you serve will wound you. You will be maligned, gossiped about, falsely accused, and your character called into question. These are givens for those enlisted in ministry. However, we have a choice: will we take up arms, or will we entrust ourselves to Him who judges righteously? Peter summarizes, "Do not return evil for evil or insult for insult, but give a blessing instead" (1 Peter 3:9). We have an example to follow in the Lord Jesus Christ. Today, lay down your feelings of injustice. Come to the High Priest who experienced these same temptations, and yet did not sin. Pray to Him, for He understands.

REFLECT

*P*raise - What Can I Praise God About Today?

_____

_____

_____

*R*eset - What Items Need a Reset in My Life Today?

_____

_____

_____

*A*sk - What Requests Could I Ask of God Today?

_____

_____

_____

*Y*ield - How Can I Assume a Posture of Submission Toward God Today?

_____

_____

_____

RECONNECT

_____

_____

_____

_____

_____

_____

DAY #19 - KEEP YOUR ANTENNAS HIGH

MATTHEW 25:35

*"For I was hungry and you gave me food,
I was thirsty and you gave me drink, I was
a stranger and you welcomed me."*

The daily grind of ministry can blind us to real Kingdom needs. We all want to be known as someone who can "get the job done." False success tells us to never get "off-task." Human achievement demands dedication and no distractions. However, ministry success is not measured in tasks completed and boxes checked. It's is a subtle, human work. Ministry is a nuanced people business. We must allow our spiritual antennae the freedom to lead us "off-task" so we can be "on-task" and "in the Spirit". Sometimes, we stop to lend a hand. Sometimes, it's a cup of cool water to a little child. Sometimes, we embrace a weary volunteer and let them know how valuable they are. *People* are His purpose. *People* are His plans. Ministry is more than tasks, duties and deadlines. It would be a shame if we climbed to the top of the ministry ladder only to realize that we placed the ladder against the wrong wall. You never know how God can use an "off-task" distraction to change the world. Keep your spiritual antennae high today.

REFLECT

*P*raise - What Can I Praise God About Today?

_____

_____

_____

*R*eset - What Items Need a Reset in My Life Today?

_____

_____

_____

*A*sk - What Requests Could I Ask of God Today?

_____

_____

_____

*Y*ield - How Can I Assume a Posture of Submission Toward God Today?

_____

_____

_____

RECONNECT

_____

_____

_____

_____

_____

_____

DAY #20 - TODAY IS A CHOICE

ROMANS 12:11
"Never be lacking in zeal, but keep your spiritual fervor, serving the Lord."

Zeal is defined as "a great energy or enthusiasm in pursuit of a cause or an objective." We are told to never be lacking in zeal. Fervor is defined as having an "intense and passionate feeling." Again, we are told to keep, or maintain, our spiritual fervor. The words "zeal" and "fervor" are less frequent in our daily language today. Though these words may be uncommon, the Scriptures make it clear that their essence should be evident in our lives. Just like our daily energy ebbs and flows, so too our zeal and spiritual fervor can be found either peaking or lacking. This verse is a reminder that we have a mission. We are here to serve the Lord. Sometimes, we sense the blessing of a real spiritual fire. Sometimes, however, we sense the numbness, chill and absence of spiritual fire. We are, as C.S. Lewis states, subject to the "Law of Undulation." We have troughs and valleys, mountaintops and peaks, in every area of our lives. We should expect this sense of up and down in our faith journey. Are you experiencing zealousness in your walk with the Lord? Do you currently have a sense of spiritual intensity or fervor? Talk to the Lord about your current state.

REFLECT

*P*raise - *What Can I Praise God About Today?*

_____

_____

_____

*R*eset - *What Items Need a Reset in My Life Today?*

_____

_____

_____

*A*sk - *What Requests Could I Ask of God Today?*

_____

_____

_____

*Y*ield - *How Can I Assume a Posture of Submission Toward God Today?*

_____

_____

_____

RECONNECT

_____

_____

_____

_____

_____

_____

PART 3

DAYS 21-30

OVERCOMING SPIRITUAL PARALYSIS

Have you ever had a feeling of spiritual paralysis? I've felt stuck. I've felt like something was wrong. It was like I was somehow out of step with the Lord. I felt a sense of being paralyzed spiritually. I have also learned how to overcome spiritual paralysis.

Unconfessed Sin

First, I ask God to search me, to know my heart, and to see if there is any offensive way within me (Psalm 139:23-24). Unconfessed sin acts as a barrier to your relationship with God. This may include a judgmental heart, a sharp tongue, a wrong thought, a wandering eye, or a prideful spirit. I record my sins. Now, I have a list to confess.

Burdens

Next, I look through my list of burdens. I mark some as "things," and others as **"things to do."** Some items weighing my heart are just "things" that I need to acknowledge are bothering me. I cannot *DO* much of anything about my nagging cold. The stack of papers on my desk is also a burden. The difference between my nagging cold (*a thing*) and that mountain of papers is (*a thing to do*) an important distinction. My "things" are often items I cannot control. "Things to do," on the other hand, are items over which I do have control.

It's good to remember that I can be in a funk even when the source of my feelings is *not* sin. Separating these two categories has been massively freeing to me. My stack of papers (a thing to do) and my sharp tongue (sin) are simply not the same. Both are adding to my sense of spiritual paralysis, but their causes, and the ways in which I deal with them, are wholly different.

Pray

Lastly, I take my entire list to prayer. I pray and confess my sin. I clear it up with the Lord. I leave it at the cross. I now pray through the "things" list, the items I cannot control. I cast my anxieties upon Him because He cares for me (1 Peter 5:7). I move forward, knowing that I've entrusted it to God and that He heard me. Then, I pray about the "things to do" list, over which I *do* have control. I ask God to empower me to accomplish these things.

Rather than sitting and feeling like a slug, I can pray, get perspective, and *get moving*. **Stress often comes not from what we are DOING, but from what we THINK we should be doing.**

It has been a great blessing to identify items that need to be confessed, items that I simply need to talk to God about, and items I need to find some diligence for and do. Who knows? This simple exercise may help you in overcoming spiritual paralysis, as well!

DAY #21 – HERE AM I, AGAIN

ISAIAH 6:8

"Then I heard the voice of the Lord, saying,
'Whom shall I send, and who will go for
Us?' Then I said, 'Here am I. Send me!'"

Isaiah's heed to the call of ministry in Isaiah chapter 6 is extreme. His commissioning is intense—an angel touched his lips with a hot and holy ember. For many of us, however, the call to ministry was far less specular and compelling. You may find yourself overseeing a large area of ministry simply because you didn't quit. You outlasted everyone else, and someone asked you to lead it all by default. Regardless of how you found yourself in the role, you said "Yes." Can I challenge you today? Would you be willing to re-accept that call? Would you be willing to officially tell the Lord that you accept this call? Could you pause, right now, and reaffirm, "Here am I, again, Lord"? Years ago, I asked a seasoned pastor, "How will I know if I am called?" His response was sobering: "If you can keep from going into the ministry, by all means, stay out. Do not enter these waters if you are not called. If you cannot keep from it, you are called." Are you ready to reaffirm your sacred calling today?

REFLECT

*P*raise - *What Can I Praise God About Today?*

_____

_____

_____

*R*eset - *What Items Need a Reset in My Life Today?*

_____

_____

_____

*A*sk - *What Requests Could I Ask of God Today?*

_____

_____

_____

*Y*ield - *How Can I Assume a Posture of Submission Toward God Today?*

_____

_____

_____

RECONNECT

_____

_____

_____

_____

_____

_____

DAY #22 – MAKING THE TEAM

LUKE 10:1-2

"After this the Lord appointed seventy-two others and sent them on ahead of him, two by two, into every town and place where he himself was about to go. And he said to them, "The harvest is plentiful, but the laborers are few. Therefore pray earnestly to the Lord of the harvest to send out laborers into his harvest."

When I was a kid, I was always picked last. I suppose I had less to contribute to the kickball universe. Sometimes, in fact, the other team would say, "You can have him," insinuating that the other team would be worse with me. Reality check: You made the team. You were picked. You are part of the team who has been sent on this mission. This mission is not a game. This is not a dress rehearsal. This is the real thing. *You are a laborer in His field.* Likely, someone prayed a prayer, asked the Lord of the harvest for workers, and you were the answer. You are on the team. I did not get picked for kickball, backyard football, or many other sports. But we made the first team in the Kingdom. Who is on your team that you need to celebrate today? Which person do you need to call? Whose presence on the team do you need to celebrate today? God has chosen the foolish things of this world and made Himself a glorious team. Rejoice!

REFLECT

*P*raise - *What Can I Praise God About Today?*

_____

_____

_____

*R*eset - *What Items Need a Reset in My Life Today?*

_____

_____

_____

*A*sk - *What Requests Could I Ask of God Today?*

_____

_____

_____

*Y*ield - *How Can I Assume a Posture of Submission Toward God Today?*

_____

_____

_____

RECONNECT

_____

_____

_____

_____

_____

_____

DAY #23 – FLIES ON THE SCREEN

PHILIPPIANS 3:1
"Finally, my brothers, rejoice in the Lord.
To write the same things to you is no
trouble to me and is safe for you."

Imagine a wonderful summer day. The sun is out. The temperature is pleasant. The screen door, however, provides a sad juxtaposition. You see the painful contrast between two flies on either side of the screen. The flies seem desperate to switch places. The fly on the inside just wants to be "out," and the fly outside just wants to be "in." I have seen ministry leaders develop a disdain for their calling and just want "out." I have also seen discontented lay leaders who want nothing more than to quit their marketplace job and be "in" ministry. I used to want "out" of my teaching job, and I wanted "in" to the ministry so badly. Now, I praise God for the sacred opportunity to serve Him vocationally. Do not allow the hardships of your calling to fuel discontentment. We get to do this thing called ministry. You get to labor for the Lord. Be happy. This life is short. Eternity awaits us. You have something that so many others only dream of having. Rejoice. Again, I will say rejoice.

REFLECT

*P*raise - What Can I Praise God About Today?

_____

_____

_____

*R*eset - What Items Need a Reset in My Life Today?

_____

_____

_____

*A*sk - What Requests Could I Ask of God Today?

_____

_____

_____

*Y*ield - How Can I Assume a Posture of Submission Toward God Today?

_____

_____

_____

RECONNECT

_____

_____

_____

_____

_____

_____

DAY #24 – MINISTRY IS A LIFESTYLE, NOT A JOB

TITUS 3:14

"Our people must learn to devote themselves to doing what is good, in order to provide for urgent needs and not live unproductive lives."

Ministry is not a 9-to-5 job. It is a calling. When viewed correctly, ministry is a lifestyle choice. The demands and duties of ministry often do not fit neatly into a Monday-through-Friday workday template. Ministry is just not that cut-and-dry. It's is not that clean and simple. Ministry is messy. As those who have taken up the mantle of ministry, we are devoted to what is good. You, oh servant, meet urgent needs. There is not a time clock, per se, in your ministry role. We do not have a "clock-in-and-clock-out" type of job. We are devoted to giving ourselves to our worthy cause. It feels good to do good. It feels good to meet an urgent need. It is a high and royal calling to lead a productive life for the Kingdom of God. Let's open our eyes today and search for to the opportunity to do what is good. Let's have an awareness of the urgent needs around us, and joyfully allow those needs to hijack today's agenda. Let's seek to live a deeply productive life. Will you pray, right now, that God would dislodge your best human plans in favor of doing *His* will today?

REFLECT

*P*raise - What Can I Praise God About Today?

_____

_____

_____

*R*eset - What Items Need a Reset in My Life Today?

_____

_____

_____

*A*sk - What Requests Could I Ask of God Today?

_____

_____

_____

*Y*ield - How Can I Assume a Posture of Submission Toward God Today?

_____

_____

_____

RECONNECT

_____

_____

_____

_____

_____

_____

DAY #25 – THE RIGHT DNA

EPHESIANS 2:10

"For we are his workmanship, created in Christ Jesus for good works, which God prepared beforehand, that we should walk in them."

Have you seen altered photos that combine two animals? Alligator-Eagle. Cat-Shark. Cheetah-Wasp. Someone altered and melded two animals into one; and yet, these modified animals are nowhere to be found in real creation. We all have wished we could adapt or change our physical bodies. If I were the Creator, I would have made Josh Denhart 3 inches taller, naturally muscular, and certainly not red-haired. If given the chance, you might choose to make some changes to yourself too, right? However, just as there is not a real-world purpose for an Alligator-Eagle, there is no purpose in creation for a 6'2", naturally muscular, blonde-haired Josh. God is a Master Builder, and we are each one-of-a-kind works of art for a reason. Apparently, God needed a 5'11", slighter-built, red-headed Josh. So that's what He made. You were created to play your special role. God preset the conditions for you to be you so that you can carry out the exact good works He prepared beforehand for you to do. He built your very DNA to pull off His will. Own that today. Can you pause and celebrate how you have been created?

REFLECT

*P*raise - What Can I Praise God About Today?

_____

_____

_____

*R*eset - What Items Need a Reset in My Life Today?

_____

_____

_____

*A*sk - What Requests Could I Ask of God Today?

_____

_____

_____

*Y*ield - How Can I Assume a Posture of Submission Toward God Today?

_____

_____

_____

RECONNECT

_____

_____

_____

_____

_____

_____

DAY #26 – KNOWING GOD THROUGH EXPERIENCE

COLOSSIANS 1:9-10
"For this reason also, since the day we heard of it, we have not ceased to pray for you and to ask that you may be filled with the knowledge of His will in all spiritual wisdom and understanding."

Paul wants believers to have "knowledge of His will in all spiritual wisdom and understanding." The Greek word Paul uses here for "knowledge" is *epignosis* (pronounced e-pē'-gnō-sēs). One can "know" (gnosis) and be acquainted with a fact. However, someone can either have "over-knowledge" or "upon-knowledge" (*epignosis*). Paul's hope is that believers would have additional, *experiential* knowledge of God's will, as opposed to strictly possessing factual knowledge. It's one thing to read and know, "God provides." It is quite another thing to experience His faithful provision in real time. I want to have both "factual" and "experiential" knowledge of the Lord. Factual knowledge learns of His promises. Deeper knowledge comes as we stand on those promises and experience His provision. This builds "upon" my factual knowing. Have you *experienced* God provide for you? If yes, you have "epi" (upon) "gnosis" (knowledge). Put some of God's promises to work today, and know Him more fully.

REFLECT

*P*raise - *What Can I Praise God About Today?*

_____

_____

_____

*R*eset - *What Items Need a Reset in My Life Today?*

_____

_____

_____

*A*sk - *What Requests Could I Ask of God Today?*

_____

_____

_____

*Y*ield - *How Can I Assume a Posture of Submission Toward God Today?*

_____

_____

_____

RECONNECT

_____

_____

_____

_____

_____

_____

DAY #27 – POWER TO PERSEVERE

COLOSSIANS 1:11
*"...strengthened with all power, according
to His glorious might, for the attaining of
all steadfastness and patience..."*

In this verse, Paul uses two variations of the same the Greek word, *dunamis* (δύναμις). *Dunamis* is the word from which we get our word "dynamite." The phrase "strengthened with all power" is literally translated, "powered for all powering." We are given, in some sense, "dynamite ability for all dynamiting." Keep in mind: the first century writers knew nothing of explosives. This word is not explosive-powering but Spirit-Powering. We all want to be em*powered*, right? We all want dynamic (same root word) strength to be given to us. But what is Paul's hope for those who have such power? Is this powering for the sake of charging ahead? No. Is it powering to be fearless? It is not. Is it powering to speak boldly? Nope. This power is allocated for "the attaining of all steadfastness and patience." I need Spirit-Power for "stick-with-it-ness." Being prone to wander, I need power to sit still and hold fast. Adherence to my call demands power from above. Today, ask God for His power to persevere.

REFLECT

Praise - What Can I Praise God About Today?

Reset - What Items Need a Reset in My Life Today?

Ask - What Requests Could I Ask of God Today?

Yield - How Can I Assume a Posture of Submission Toward God Today?

RECONNECT

DAY #28 – DON'T BE A BALL HOG

HEBREWS 13:16

***"Do not neglect to do good and to share what you
have, for such sacrifices are pleasing to God."***

I was an elementary P.E. teacher for one semester. We played
a two-team variation of dodgeball called "Bombardment,"
using eight foam balls for ammunition. I will never forget a
kid named Forest. His strategy was clear: Hold as many balls
as his arms would allow. Forest stockpiled ammunition in his
chubby arms, thinking this gave him an advantage. It did not.
His team suffered. He became a sitting duck as he clumsily
attempted to hold a fourth ball. Forest was a ball hog. It hurt
him. It hurt his team. Learn from Forest's simple mistake. Don't
be a leadership hog. Do not be a service hoarder. Do you
tightly hold tasks, mistakenly thinking that you are "saving volunteers from extra work?" Sharing the work brings blessing to
volunteers, both now and in the afterlife. What kingdom tasks
are you hoarding that might rob someone of laying up treasures in heaven? When you share the opportunity to lay up
treasure, you get treasure in heaven, as well. Try this today.

REFLECT

*P*raise - What Can I Praise God About Today?

_____

_____

_____

*R*eset - What Items Need a Reset in My Life Today?

_____

_____

_____

*A*sk - What Requests Could I Ask of God Today?

_____

_____

_____

*Y*ield - How Can I Assume a Posture of Submission Toward God Today?

_____

_____

_____

RECONNECT

_____

_____

_____

_____

_____

_____

DAY #29 – WHO GETS THE GLORY?

MATTHEW 5:16

"In the same way, let your light shine before others, so that they may see your good works and give glory to your Father who is in heaven."

As one who has served for years in ministry, I know what it is like. Our efforts in ministry can be given with right motives. However, they can also be for self-exaltation. Your good works *are* shining. However, it's a matter of *who* gets the spotlight. When we serve with a pure heart, God gets glory. Our good works can be evidence that points toward God. On the other hand, our good works can crave the spotlight, wanting all eyes to be on us. God wants our good works to be seen. He wants them to be placed upon a hilltop. He wants them put on a stand for all to see and benefit from. But the goal and benefit in them is that people will see *the Lord* more clearly. Would you feel jealous if your efforts were utterly unnoticed and yet, as a result, someone longed more for God? Sadly, my head knows the right answer, but my heart wants credit on earth. Today, be mindful of the motivation behind your good works. Assume a mental posture that allows others to see good works and associate those works with God's love for them.

REFLECT

*P*raise - *What Can I Praise God About Today?*

_____

_____

_____

*R*eset - *What Items Need a Reset in My Life Today?*

_____

_____

_____

*A*sk - *What Requests Could I Ask of God Today?*

_____

_____

_____

*Y*ield - *How Can I Assume a Posture of Submission Toward God Today?*

_____

_____

_____

RECONNECT

_____

_____

_____

_____

_____

_____

DAY #30 — EVERY SINGLE THING

I CORINTHIANS 15:58
"Therefore, my beloved brethren, be steadfast, immovable, always abounding in the work of the Lord, knowing that your toil is not in vain in the Lord."

Ministry is filled with the most random tasks and "duties as assigned." Those not in full-time ministry jokingly say, "Well, all you do is work on Sunday, right?" Far be it! Early on in my decade-long tenure as a pastor, I adopted this verse: "... knowing that nothing you do in the Lord is in vain." I kept this passage on the forefront of my mind. I allowed it to be quick off my tongue. Honestly, I needed it. I needed to remember that even particularly obscure and never-to-be-seen tasks hold value in the Lord. I desperately wanted to be abounding in the work of the Lord, yet I never could have imagined some of the bizarre things I would need to do. Remember, your toil in the Lord is *not* in vain ... and toil it often is. Enter this day with a singular mindset: *My work matters.* Embrace your toil with this frame of mind. Adopt an attitude of the heart that pushes every boulder, rock, or pebble as unto the Lord, knowing that these things truly do matter. Today, you will do some less-than-glamorous tasks. Be steadfast—immovable—and abound in this, His, work today.

REFLECT

*P*raise - What Can I Praise God About Today?

_____

_____

_____

*R*eset - What Items Need a Reset in My Life Today?

_____

_____

_____

*A*sk - What Requests Could I Ask of God Today?

_____

_____

_____

*Y*ield - How Can I Assume a Posture of Submission Toward God Today?

_____

_____

_____

RECONNECT

_____

_____

_____

_____

_____

_____

PART 4

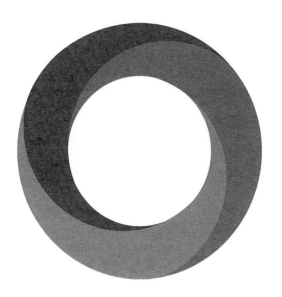

DAYS 31-40

THE HARVEST IS PLENTIFUL

The harvest is plentiful, the workers are few. Ask the Lord of the harvest to send out workers.

Have you ever felt weighed down under the pressure of your workload and the mountain of volunteers you need to find? What do you do in this situation? I honestly, and shamefully, must admit that, at times, I haven't prayed and asked God for His help and His leading. Often, I have taken on the task of recruiting apart from Jesus, not stopping to pray to the Lord of the harvest. My question to you is this: are you praying and asking God for more volunteers, or recruiting on your own?

Pray to the Lord of the Harvest

In Matthew 9, Jesus approaches his disciples and says, "Look at the fields. They are ripe for harvest." He says to ask the Lord of the harvest, the boss of this field, to send out workers to help collect it. "The harvest is plentiful, but the workers are few. Therefore, ask the Lord of the harvest to send workers into his field." Notice that, as soon as that phrase is uttered, we enter a new chapter. Not only do we enter into chapter 10 of Matthew, but we actually enter into a brand new chapter in the life and ministry of Jesus. As soon as He says this phrase, Jesus does the very thing He had asked others to do. The Bible says in Matthew 10:1 that Jesus went away to a solitary place and prayed all night long. He asked God which of the 120 followers He should choose to be in His exclusive group of 12 disciples.

The Bible says Jesus came down from the mountain and chose the twelve. I want you to understand that Jesus went to the mountain and specifically prayed to God the Father to raise up the right twelve. He was praying for the men that would carry out and carry on the work after His crucifixion and resurrection. After that prayer, Jesus chose these men.

Ask God

I will ask you again: are you praying and asking God for more volunteers, or recruiting on your own? We should not only follow Jesus's instruction, but we should also follow His example. You see, it's His field. Jesus cares about it far more than we do. So shouldn't I ask Him to help find and enlist the right people to bring about a wonderful, beautiful harvest?

Remember, God does not shame you when you ask. In fact, He is pleased when you do! Are you asking for more laborers? Jesus has told us to do just this. He Himself went up to a mountain and spent the entire night beseeching God for wisdom when it came to choosing His closest group of harvesters. How much more should we do the same?

Truly, have you prayed today for God to raise up workers for the harvest? The harvest is plentiful, but the workers are few. There is no reason you need to take on this burden alone. Ask the Lord of the harvest.

DAY #31 – HOME BASE

1 CORINTHIANS 16:14
"Let all that you do be done in love."

There is work to be done. We have tasks today, big and small, which are mission-critical. Ministry is not all thought and feeling. Far be it! Ministry is not sitting and reading the Bible for eight hours a day. Those on the front lines of ministry know this is an active endeavor. Most missions have a home base. In battle, a home base is the safe place from where we begin. Home base is where we fall back. Home base is where we collect our thoughts, recalibrate our tools, and remember our why. The home base from which our tasks are derived is *love*. Our home base is neither achievement nor activity for activity's sake. Our ambition is not building an "earthly ministry/business plan." It all starts with love. As your hand hits the plow today, center yourself in Kingdom Love. Today, you may oil the gears of ministry; do it with love. You might do fourteen never-to-be seen tasks; do them with love. You may find yourself doing a Kingdom task that seems more Kingdom-mundane than Kingdom-critical. Approach all that your hand touches from a home base of love.

REFLECT

*P*raise - What Can I Praise God About Today?

_____

_____

_____

*R*eset - What Items Need a Reset in My Life Today?

_____

_____

_____

*A*sk - What Requests Could I Ask of God Today?

_____

_____

_____

*Y*ield - How Can I Assume a Posture of Submission Toward God Today?

_____

_____

_____

RECONNECT

_____

_____

_____

_____

_____

_____

DAY #32 – THE GRAVITAS OF ACTION

1 JOHN 3:18

"Dear children, let us not love with words
or speech but with actions and in truth."

It is impossible to *not* communicate; however, we *can* communicate poorly. We've all heard it said that actions speak louder than words. Even the same words with a variation of body language can have different meanings. Words are cheap,. I can and have said many things; yet good intentions and quick words are nothing compared to actions and deeds. Actions take an entirely different level of commitment and hold far greater gravitas. Your actions are communicating. The question is, *what* are they communicating? Love, they say, is a verb. Love does. It's an action word. What actions might you take today to express love and sacrifice for another? Picking up the phone is an action. Sending a heart-felt, handwritten card is an action. Surprising someone with a gift, albeit small, at his or her front door is an action. Talk is cheap. Actions simply cost more. Pray about what you can do to express love to one key person or volunteer today. Ask God to open your eyes. Ponder what step you might take today to express love as an action.

REFLECT

*P*raise - What Can I Praise God About Today?

_____

_____

_____

*R*eset - What Items Need a Reset in My Life Today?

_____

_____

_____

*A*sk - What Requests Could I Ask of God Today?

_____

_____

_____

*Y*ield - How Can I Assume a Posture of Submission Toward God Today?

_____

_____

_____

RECONNECT

_____

_____

_____

_____

_____

_____

DAY #33- BEING A BUILDER

ROMANS 15:2
"We should help others do what is right and build them up in the Lord."

Paul calls us "builders." We are following in the footsteps of the Great Carpenter, Jesus Christ. We do not carve stones. We likely don't use a hammer, a chisel, or a saw in our ministry labors. We are builders, nonetheless. We are called to lead others into what is right, and thus, to build them up. We are called to be builders of people, not buildings. The Lord Jesus is the "general contractor," overseeing the hopeful development of His children. You are a "sub-contractor," given a small portion of the work. Do you know your part of the work? Your job is not a program director. Your job is not a keeper of the schedule. Your job is not a curator of creative curriculum. Your job is to build people and help them to do what is right. As you enlist someone into the work, they, through your tender care, are built up. Often, it is through someone's participation in the work of the ministry that they grow in the Lord. Who are you leading to do what is right? Who are you building up in the Lord? Ask God for spiritual bricks and mortar today. What small step can you take, today, to lay an important brick in someone else's spiritual house?

REFLECT

*P*raise - What Can I Praise God About Today?

_____

_____

_____

*R*eset - What Items Need a Reset in My Life Today?

_____

_____

_____

*A*sk - What Requests Could I Ask of God Today?

_____

_____

_____

*Y*ield - How Can I Assume a Posture of Submission Toward God Today?

_____

_____

_____

RECONNECT

_____

_____

_____

_____

_____

_____

DAY #34 – GOD DOES NOT FORGET

HEBREWS 6:10
"God is not unjust; he will not forget your work and the love you have shown him as you have helped his people and continue to help them."

God sees, God knows and God is waiting with reward for you. He is NOT unjust! God does not forget. While you have likely forgotten some of your own times of faithfulness and labor, the Lord has not. God is all-knowing (omniscient). God is all-powerful (omnipotent). God is everywhere (omnipresent). We are omni-nothing. God is omni-everything. He sees all. He remembers all His children's works. Worship Him, because He does NOT forget our labors. We as humans, however, do forget. We have all overlooked a volunteer's labor and their contributions. Sometimes and somehow, our best volunteers' efforts have sadly gone unnoticed by us. But God, being good, does not forget our work for the Kingdom. None of our efforts in the Lord are unaccounted for or missed. Who should you pour into today, knowing that God will never forget how you seek to help the saints? In addition, who should you call today to thank for their labors in the Lord? Someone may need reminding that God has been noticing and keeping track of all their love and labor!

REFLECT

*P*raise - *What Can I Praise God About Today?*

_____

_____

_____

*R*eset - *What Items Need a Reset in My Life Today?*

_____

_____

_____

*A*sk - *What Requests Could I Ask of God Today?*

_____

_____

_____

*Y*ield - *How Can I Assume a Posture of Submission Toward God Today?*

_____

_____

_____

RECONNECT

_____

_____

_____

_____

_____

_____

DAY #35 – A LOVELY REPUTATION

JOHN 13:34-35
"A new commandment I give to you, that you love one another: just as I have loved you, you also are to love one another. By this all people will know that you are my disciples, if you have love for one another."

I am a student of people. People give us clues about their emotional state, or what they value. I notice when people who always wear contact lenses show up to a meeting wearing glasses: *Did they have a rough morning?* I notice when normally gregarious people choose a more reserved posture. It registers to me when someone consistently and quietly removes dirty dishes from others. I notice the small things. Everyone is constantly communicating, though words may not ever be used. Jesus says that love is a dead giveaway that you are His follower. A constant aura of love and self-sacrifice is rare. Love (or the lack thereof) provides an unmistakable clue to someone's spiritual condition. Reputation is earned through time + consistency of behavior. You have a reputation. You have earned it. Today, you will reinforce your reputation, one way or another. Is there a tangible way you can share love today? How might you reinforce the reality that God is Love through a singular action today?

REFLECT

*P*raise - What Can I Praise God About Today?

_____

_____

_____

*R*eset - What Items Need a Reset in My Life Today?

_____

_____

_____

*A*sk - What Requests Could I Ask of God Today?

_____

_____

_____

*Y*ield - How Can I Assume a Posture of Submission Toward God Today?

_____

_____

_____

RECONNECT

_____

_____

_____

_____

_____

_____

DAY #36 – WORK TAKES WORK

1 CORINTHIANS 3:9
***"For we are God's fellow workers. You
are God's field, God's building."***

We are in ministry. Therefore, we are workers for God's Kingdom. We are not merely spectators. We have stepped into the call. This is our vocation, but this is also our volition. This is our work, and we are in willful agreement. We *get* to do this. We are workers in God's field and we are working for a great harvest. We are *His* workers. But don't be fooled. Work takes...well...work! Ministry is hard. Sometimes, we feel worn and isolated. We feel alone and confused. You are not alone as a ministry laborer. You are a part of a great heritage of men and women who have pushed, pulled, and plowed for the Lord. We are in this together. I wouldn't want to do it alone and I wouldn't want you to think that you are doing it alone. We are *fellow* workers. We are a part of a secret and sacred club of those who know both the joys and toils of serving the Kingdom. We are here to build truth into the lives of others; and yet isolation tells us we are laboring alone. Can you reach out to a fellow laborer today and remind yourselves that you're in this together?

REFLECT

*P*raise - *What Can I Praise God About Today?*

_____

_____

_____

*R*eset - *What Items Need a Reset in My Life Today?*

_____

_____

_____

*A*sk - *What Requests Could I Ask of God Today?*

_____

_____

_____

*Y*ield - *How Can I Assume a Posture of Submission Toward God Today?*

_____

_____

_____

RECONNECT

_____

_____

_____

_____

_____

_____

DAY #37 – KNOW THE RIGHT THINGS

JOHN 13:1-4

"Jesus, knowing that the Father had given all things into his hands, and that he had come from God and was going back to God, rose from supper. He laid aside his outer garments, and taking a towel, tied it around his waist. Then he poured water into a basin and began to wash the disciples' feet and to wipe them with the towel that was wrapped around him."

Jesus knew who He was. He knew His position. He knew His purpose. Jesus knew the guarantee of His future. What about you? Whose are you? Do you know to Whom you belong? Do you know your specific and sanctioned station of ministry—your calling? Do you understand the solid footing upon which you stand? Do you grasp that nothing will remove your name from the Lamb's Book of Life? It was out of a firm understanding of these things that Jesus took that next step: Taking Up the Towel. It was His clear understanding that allowed Him to do what seemed unthinkable: wash dirty feet. Start today by reviewing the fact that you are God's child. Begin by rethinking what you have been asked to do. Center yourself by knowing where you will ultimately end up. Taking today's next step will be easier.

REFLECT

Praise - What Can I Praise God About Today?

_____

_____

_____

Reset - What Items Need a Reset in My Life Today?

_____

_____

_____

Ask - What Requests Could I Ask of God Today?

_____

_____

_____

Yield - How Can I Assume a Posture of Submission Toward God Today?

_____

_____

_____

RECONNECT

_____

_____

_____

_____

_____

_____

DAY #38 – FAITHFUL IN LITTLE

LUKE 16:10
*"He who is faithful in a very little
thing is faithful also in much."*

Ministry is a series of opportunities. Every day, we have Kingdom tasks before us. How we approach today's tasks is a telltale indicator of whether we can be trusted with tomorrow's. Here's an inescapable truth: If today, you apply excellence in seemingly insignificant tasks, you will likely apply excellence in clearly significant tasks tomorrow. If you work with a slack hand today, chances are you will work with a slack hand tomorrow. This verse is not a means of "how to climb the ministry ladder" with your human bosses. God is the one who sees and provides greater Kingdom opportunities. God quietly observes your faithful or haphazard execution. It is the Lord who recognizes your secret motivation, your love for people, and your love for the Kingdom. Your approach today will determine your future opportunities. Polish today's tiny tasks, and see what your tomorrow brings. Which of today's duties demands your special attention? Which task today can be approached "as unto the King?"

REFLECT

*P*raise - What Can I Praise God About Today?

_____

_____

_____

*R*eset - What Items Need a Reset in My Life Today?

_____

_____

_____

*A*sk - What Requests Could I Ask of God Today?

_____

_____

_____

*Y*ield - How Can I Assume a Posture of Submission Toward God Today?

_____

_____

_____

RECONNECT

_____

_____

_____

_____

_____

_____

DAY #39 – MUSCLE MEMORY

PHILIPPIANS 4:12-13
"I know what it is to be in need, and I know what it is to have plenty. I have learned the secret of being content in any and every situation, whether well fed or hungry, whether living in plenty or in want. I can do all this through him who gives me strength."

Paul can proclaim *future* "do-ability" through *previous* experience. Paul had *previous* experiences of being in need and of having plenty. Therefore, Paul convinced himself of his *future* ability to "do all things," based out of the *previous* track record of a faithful God. There is a wisdom that must be experienced *before* we can confidently state that we "can do all future things" through Christ who gives us strength. One must have experienced a secret contentment when outside things looked bleak. One must have mastered this secret contentment, also, when blessings abounded. Paul had a spiritual "muscle memory" that allowed him to confidently face the unknown in his future. God has provided me with "mission success" both when I had an abundance of well-qualified volunteers and when I felt woefully understaffed. Therefore, the future seems brighter because of my rearview mirror. Look back today, and reflect.

REFLECT

*P*raise - What Can I Praise God About Today?

_____

_____

_____

*R*eset - What Items Need a Reset in My Life Today?

_____

_____

_____

*A*sk - What Requests Could I Ask of God Today?

_____

_____

_____

*Y*ield - How Can I Assume a Posture of Submission Toward God Today?

_____

_____

_____

RECONNECT

_____

_____

_____

_____

_____

_____

DAY #40 – THE DOUBLE BONUS

2 CORINTHIANS 9:12
"...this service is not only supplying the needs of the saints but is also overflowing in many thanksgivings to God."

Our ministry is rendered unto God, not to people. Plainly stated, we serve God, not man. However, our labors in the Lord do meet the needs of other human beings...it just doesn't end there. There is an easily overlooked "spiritual bonus" that results from our efforts. Consider this: People, whose needs are met by you might thank God for what you did. God not only gains glory as (1) you selflessly serve Him, but as He receives (2) offerings of thanks from those whose needs are met. Here's the basic rundown: First, you serve God. Second, your service meets someone's need. Third, God received heartfelt worship through thanks from the one whose needs were met. I know this sounds elemental and basic; yet it brings me joy to consider that someone might report thanks to our Dad for what you have done. There is an amazing double bonus: (1) God gets your sacrifice *and* (2) someone else's thanks. Today, render your service not for the applause of men. Instead, bless others, and they might tell our Father than you for helping them: double win.

REFLECT

*P*raise - What Can I Praise God About Today?

_____

_____

_____

*R*eset - What Items Need a Reset in My Life Today?

_____

_____

_____

*A*sk - What Requests Could I Ask of God Today?

_____

_____

_____

*Y*ield - How Can I Assume a Posture of Submission Toward God Today?

_____

_____

_____

RECONNECT

_____

_____

_____

_____

_____

_____

CONCLUSION: NO NEED FOR ANXIETY

Don't be anxious. In the book of Philippians, the apostle Paul gives us some pretty challenging words: "Do not argue or complain about anything" (Philippians 2:14).

Interestingly enough, this verse can easily be applied to our work as parents. Think about it: I have four kids. my kids are pretty quick to complain. My kids are pretty quick to argue with each other and with me. Let's take a look at ourselves. How about me? How about you? If I'm honest with myself, I complain quite a bit, about a great deal of things. Honestly, I complain quite a bit about my kids! "Too loud. Disobeying. Not listening." The list of complaints goes on.

Let's take this verse at face value. Let's say I completely stop verbally complaining and arguing. What then? Well, if I were to be honest with myself, the complaints that I resist coming out of my mouth will probably still be brewing deep inside of my heart and soul. While I might be able to keep myself from arguing or complaining *out loud*, the issue could still be quite unsettled in my heart.

While it's a good thing to not verbally argue or complain, what does a follower of Christ do with that internal tension that exists in your heart? Most of us forget that the letter to the Philippians was written as a complete letter. It did not have verses, and it did not have chapter breaks. When Paul tells us not to argue or complain, he also gives us the means of doing so, the remedy, in the very same letter.

You see, Paul addresses this exact question later in the book where he shares, "Do not be anxious about anything, but in everything, by prayer and petition, present your requests to God; and the peace of God which transcends all understanding will guard your hearts and your minds in Christ Jesus" (Philippians 4:6-7).

Have you ever experienced a troublesome day as a parent—a day in which you just felt like nothing was working right? Frustration mounted. Maybe you even experienced a loss of joy and a feeling of anxious dread. Factor in the to-dos: the lawn needs mowed. The laundry never ceases. The kids have not been bathed in way too long. It's a tough challenge, being a mom or a dad. Yet rather than fret about it, complain about it, or argue about it, surrender these requests to God. He hears.

Do you have tension in your life? Take God at His word. Rather than audibly bellyaching, which is often my first response, I challenge all of us today to take the next step, as suggested by God in his Word, and share that anxiety with God through prayer.